This scary
book belongs to:

Halloween Party
Costume Coloring Book

Mary Lou Brown & Sandy Mahony

adventurelearningpress.com

www.ingramcontent.com/pod-product-compliance
Lightning Source LLC
Chambersburg PA
CBHW081807280526
45789CB00008B/3035